HOME OFFICE RESEARCH STUDY NO. 55

Crime Prevention and the Police

By John Burrows, Paul Ekblom and Kevin Heal

A HOME OFFICE
RESEARCH UNIT
REPORT

LONDON: HER MAJESTY'S STATIONERY OFFICE

HOME OFFICE RESEARCH STUDIES

'Home Office Research Studies' comprise reports on research undertaken in the Home Office to assist in the exercise of its administrative functions, and for the information of the judicature, the services for which the Home Secretary has responsibility (direct or indirect) and the general public.

On the last pages of this report are listed titles already published in this series, and in the preceding series *Studies in the Causes of Delinquency and the Treatment of Offenders.*

ISBN 0 11 340695 9

Foreword

The prevention of crime involves more than the traditional police patrol. In recent years many schemes have been mounted by the police, some with the aim of reducing crime through increasing community commitment, others with the object of encouraging the public to take greater care of their property. Some success has been claimed for a number of these activities; however, few have been the subject of rigorous evaluation so that the widely held belief in their efficacy remains to be substantiated. The studies reported in this volume, both experimental in design, examine two aspects of crime prevention and assess their impact on particular types of crime.

The first study examines the effectiveness of a publicity campaign to encourage the public to lock unattended vehicles and so reduce car crime. It shows that the publicity affected neither drivers' propensity to lock their vehicles, nor the incidence of car theft.

The effectiveness of truancy patrols in reducing crimes committed by children was the subject of the second study. There was little convincing evidence that the patrols cut crime at times when children should have been at school—indeed, the amount of offending attributable to those playing truant appeared small. The study was not able, however, to illuminate the longer-term preventive effects of the patrols or other benefits that may have accrued for the police in the form, for example, of improved relations with schools and the public.

Thus, while there is a clear need for further examination of these and other aspects of crime prevention, the studies reported in this volume provide no evidence to suggest that either of the two separate initiatives described led to a reduction in the level of reported crime; the authors of the report offer some explanation of why this should be so.

I. J. CROFT
Head of the Research Unit

June 1979

Acknowledgements

Thanks are due to the officers of Devon and Cornwall Constabulary for their co-operation in the study of police publicity. In particular we would like to thank Brian Morgan, Assistant Chief Constable, for his advice and guidance in setting up the study, and John Bastone, Bernard Lindsell and John Tarr who with their colleagues offered every assistance in its conduct. We are grateful also to Mike Hough and other members of the staff of the Home Office Research Unit who took part in the vehicle check and interview stages of the research.

The truancy study owes much to the Chief Constable of Avon and Somerset, for enabling it to be carried out, and to John Gaut and Philip Veater of the crime prevention department, for their considerable help. We are indebted, too, to Martin Watts, principal education welfare officer of Avon, for co-operating in the exercise and providing much useful information and advice. Thanks must go also to the general manager, the security manager and the staff of the store in which counts of children were made, and to the detectives from the other stores who kept records for us.

JOHN BURROWS

PAUL EKBLOM

KEVIN HEAL

Contents

I Police Car Security Campaigns

by John Burrows and Kevin Heal

INTRODUCTION

Many police forces meet their responsibility for crime prevention by mounting publicity campaigns designed to inform people about the risk of crime and the steps that can be taken to prevent it. The study described here examines the effectiveness of a publicity campaign designed to encourage car drivers to lock up their vehicles.

Two basic assumptions underlie car security campaigns: first, that drivers who leave their vehicles unlocked invite theft, and second, that by disseminating information about the risk of theft, drivers can be persuaded to take more care to protect their vehicles. If publicity is to continue to play a central role in a bid to prevent crime it is clearly important to consider the validity of these assumptions.

Car security publicity is disseminated from two sources: from the police, and from the Home Office. Campaigns conducted by the police are typically local events, organised on relatively low budgets, but taking considerable advantage of the willingness of local authorities, firms, and news media to disseminate public service advice at little or no cost. With obvious reason, evaluations of police campaigns—mostly carried out by crime prevention officers themselves—have looked at the effect of publicity on levels of reported crime, though sometimes changes in drivers' car locking behaviour have been monitored. Home Office campaigns, in contrast, are conducted by professional advertising agents at considerably greater cost; the task of evaluation here generally falls to market research organisations. The evaluation of the 1976 Home Office national campaign, unlike those undertaken by the police, was concerned primarily with the impact of publicity on drivers' attitudes and their knowledge of the risk of vehicle theft.

A considerable number of police campaigns are reported to have been successful in reducing autocrime[1], for example, those in Sunderland (Sunderland Crime Prevention Panel, 1975), Southampton (Home Office, 1974), the West Midlands (Home Office, 1976) and Bolton (Home Office, 1975) are said to have reduced vehicle theft by varying degrees. However, in those instances where changes in drivers' locking behaviour have been evaluated as a measure of effectiveness, the evidence is conflicting. A short campaign of intensive publicity in Sheffield failed to raise the number of locked cars (Bright, 1967), whereas campaigns in Nottingham (Home Office, 1974) and Bath (Home Office, 1975) are reported to have met some success in achieving this objective.

A central difficulty in attempting to evaluate publicity in terms of its effect on crime arises from the need to predict normal variations in crime during a

---

[1] Autocrime is defined in this, and the following report as taking and driving away, and theft from and of vehicles.

campaign, so that changes occurring outside this range can be attributed to the police activity in question. Few evaluations of police campaigns recognise the complexity of this problem: as a result, campaigns are conducted without controlling or taking into account extraneous influences on crime. Moreover, autocrime statistics are analysed without reference either to the changing pattern of other property offences in the vicinity, or to the incidence of car crime in comparable non-campaign areas.

Those studies which have investigated the influence of campaigns on drivers' propensity to lock their vehicles when leaving them unattended have similar drawbacks. From the information available, it appears that most police checks are made without any considered decision about either what sampling techniques are to be employed, or what steps are required to ensure comparability between samples. Nor is there evidence regarding the precautions taken to reduce the visibility of those carrying out checks, and so avoid the likelihood that these measure the public response to the checks themselves in preference to the publicity[1], Bright's Sheffield evaluation, though in other respects a careful study, was based on an uncommonly low level of pre-campaign insecurity (6%)[2], probably arrived at because in place of a single 'snapshot', security was determined by a large series of conspicuous police checks in the same area. Furthermore, few evaluations encompass a series of checks designed to identify how rapidly car drivers respond to police advice and the duration of this effect.

The results of previous evaluative efforts, therefore, offer no clear indication as to the effectiveness of police advertising campaigns. Similarly, the results of the 1976 national campaign have been subject to various interpretations. There is evidence that this campaign, conducted at a cost of some £250,000, led to an improvement in drivers' attitudes to car locking, and to drivers' knowledge of the risk of car theft (Research Bureau Limited, 1977), but, from the relatively small-scale survey of vehicles carried out, it appears that this desired improvement in attitude was not translated into improved locking behaviour. There is, moreover, no clear evidence that car theft was reduced as a result of the campaign: there was a minor fall in the incidence of offences of theft and unauthorised taking during 1976, but there is no strong evidence to support the view that this should be attributed to the campaign. The fact that some comparable property crimes remained stable in 1976, and that vehicle thefts were higher during the campaign quarter than in the preceding quarters, seems rather to contradict this explanation.

---

[1] Of course the police may use vehicle checks to publicise the extent of vehicle insecurity; reference here is to checks carried out purely for evaluative purposes.

[2] This was certainly lower than any level recorded by campaign evaluators in similar pre-campaign daylight checks: Research Bureau Limited (1977) found 35% of the vehicles they checked insecure in some way, and the police in the Nottingham area showed 'an average as high as 37 to 40% vehicles were left insecure' prior to the campaign in this area (Home Office, 1974).

The study reported below seeks to explore the same questions as these previous evaluative efforts, but under more rigorous research conditions. Its aim was to examine, by means of controlled experiment, the effectiveness of a typical police campaign both in reducing car crime and in improving drivers' locking habits. It was thought necessary to take account of crime statistics as well as levels of security since, even if the latter did not improve, crime levels might have declined as a result of potential offenders being deterred by the attention given to autocrime.

EXPERIMENTAL CAMPAIGN

The value of the controlled experiment has been widely discussed by both criminological (e.g. Clarke and Cornish, 1972) and advertising research (e.g. Bloom and Twyman, 1978) authorities. The experiment described here shares many of the charactertistics, and the difficulties, associated with this type of research, above all the need to control for extraneous variables likely to influence the results obtained; in contrast, however, there has been little need to come to terms with many of the critical issues of design and methodology particular to more complex experiments. Thus, to take an example, while penologists have to consider the variety of aims served by penal treatments, the police aim in mounting security publicity is not so diffuse, the behavioural response of the public quite easily monitored, and—in place of the more intractable ethical and practical problems involved in allocating offenders to different treatment—the research has to face the less complicated task of randomly sampling vehicles during checks carried out in the campaign area.

The controlled experiment has, of course, been used a great deal to measure the effect of advertising campaigns (see Caffyn, 1977). It has been pointed out, nonetheless, that it is inappropriate to undertake short-term evaluations in certain circumstances, for such studies are not a reliable means of measuring long-term effects (particularly in the case of campaigns dealing with themes of sustained public concern, such as smoking), or of effects apparent only after a lapse of time (the 'sleeper' effect).

For a number of reasons, these arguments were thought to carry less weight with regard to police campaigns designed to promote car security. Although campaigns of this nature may be an enduring aspect of the crime prevention officer's work, in any one area this matter is only publicised occasionally; the issue, therefore, receives only irregular publicity that is unlikely to produce a gradual change in public attitudes. There appears, moreover, to be little reason why any effects of these campaigns should be delayed; whereas the smoker, when short of money or ill, may have cause to reconsider his initial negative reactions to publicity, the car driver is passed only a simple message, and is likely only to reconsider his initial negative reaction after he or an acquaintance become victims of theft themselves.

The most common charge, however, to be made against publicity experiments of any type is that general implications cannot be drawn from the findings of any one study, for the response of the public is largely dictated by the creative content of advertising material and campaign expenditure levels. Although the apparently contradictory results of research on other social persuasion campaigns stand witness to the validity of this assertion, it is held here that in the case of car security campaigns it has less force. Notwithstanding the occasional publicity gimmick produced by the police to highlight the issue, most campaigns conducted by the police vary little either in the media sources used or in the message transmitted, and in the majority of cases forces use the same publicity material provided free by the Home Office. The principal objective of the experiment described here was to evaluate a police campaign conducted along these conventional lines.

CHARACTERISTICS OF THE CAMPAIGN

The campaign was conducted in Plymouth (population 300,000, approximately) over a five week period between mid-November and mid-December 1977. Although not excessive by the standards of some other cities of comparable size, its level of autocrime was seen by the police to be one of its more pressing problems[1]. Several features of the city made it an excellent site for the experiment: it coincides with a single police division with an active crime prevention department, and—possessing an independent radio station together with two daily and two weekly newspapers, each enthusiastic to assist police efforts—it offered a wide range of outlets by which the campaign message could be disseminated.

In order to satisfy the requirements of the sampling design (discussed below), a great deal of the campaign publicity was concentrated within the high-risk areas for autocrime offences. These were identified by an analysis of autocrime in the area carried out before the campaign; the areas selected comprised approximately one third of the city, and included the whole of the city centre; within the selected areas the police distributed posters and handbills. In addition, extensive coverage of the campaign was provided by the press, the local radio station, and television, by which means the campaign message was disseminated well outside the city boundaries. It was assumed that those resident in the central area, subject to the publicity from each of these sources, would be those most aware of the existence of the campaign.

Publicity material from all these sources was devised with a view to gaining maximum impact of the campaign message; it referred to the level of crime in the locality, the high risk points, the types of vehicle at risk, notable instances of car crime recently reported to the police, and to the negligence of many victims. The publicity generated by both the media and the police was considerable: total press coverage for the campaign comprised 109 column inches, much of it headline space, and radio/TV coverage ranged from short

---

In 1977, 1,035 unauthorised takings and thefts of vehicles, and 973 thefts from vehicles, came to the notice of the police in the city division.

5

mentions in news bulletins to a 'talk-in' programme involving crime prevention officers. A total of 5,000 handbills were distributed (outlets ranging from garages and motorists' spare parts shops to clubs and post offices); over 140 posters were placed at strategic points in central car parks (particularly close to payment meters) and garages; and the 'talking car', a vehicle used by the police to publicise crime prevention advice[1], toured central areas on five occasions.

The cost of the campaign is difficult to assess. The local media offered extensive editorial and programme support free of charge[2], on condition that the information was newsworthy. The direct cost of the campaign to the police was therefore nominal, and was restricted primarily to charges made for the printing of posters and handbills. Indirect costs, of police time engaged in making arrangements for publicity, distributing advertising material, or manning the 'talking car', were undoubtedly the principal component of the total cost incurred. Four divisional crime prevention officers were engaged in varying degrees for the duration of the campaign, as was—to a lesser extent—the time of crime prevention officers and press officers at the police headquarters.

METHOD OF EVALUATION

Two measures were used to monitor the impact of the campaign: levels of car security, and autocrime statistics. These are discussed in turn.

Security levels

In order to measure changes in the level of car security, checks were carried out at various stages of the campaign. These were made by four teams comprising one uniformed policeman and one researcher; they were carried out:

i. on the day preceding the start of the campaign[3];

ii. at the close of the second week;

iii. at the close of the fourth week; and

iv. at the end of the campaign.

Each check was conducted along the same route in the high risk central area of

---

[1] The 'talking car' is fitted with most available security devices, and a public address system. Manned by a police officer, it is generally employed in busy shopping or office areas to provide the public with security advice.

[2] This is not always the case in metropolitan areas primarily because of the increased cost of news space and the fact that other local news is likely to be more sensational. The 1977/78 Metropolitan Police security campaign, for example, incurred a bill of £96,000 (direct cost alone).

[3] Despite careful briefing of the police, two newspapers and the local radio station gave premature notice that the police intended to conduct a campaign. The police were able to prevent further publication, and the amount published amounted to little more than a routine reminder to the public of the dangers of leaving their cars unlocked.

he city and covered 1,000 cars or non-commercial light vans parked there, an estimated 5% of those in the area[1].

For a number of reasons—not least that the majority of autocrime offences are carried out under cover of darkness—these checks were conducted in the evening between the hours of 6 and 10 p.m. This reduced the visibility of the police officers carrying out the checks and the impact their activity might have had on drivers' behaviour. Each police/researcher team was allocated a fixed route measuring approximately four miles, along which they checked the doors, windows and boots of 250 vehicles. In the absence of detailed local authority plans showing the distribution of vehicles in the evening period, each pair was directed to make a random selection of the vehicles checked. There were two constraints on this selection: a predetermined number of vehicles were to be selected from designated car parks along the route (the capacity of the park dictating the numbers chosen), and each route was divided into five equal sections, from each of which 50 vehicles were to be checked. Teams finding vehicles insecure were directed to record the make, model and registration details of that vehicle, the source of insecurity, and its parking location.

On the third check the teams recorded these details for all the vehicles checked (whether insecure or not). The information gathered enabled the researchers to distinguish the respects in which vehicles left insecure differed from those locked. In addition, by this means it was possible to confirm that the vehicle sample covered a representative cross section of cars in the area.

Autocrime statistics

The crime statistics analysed were principally drawn from the records of offences known to the police. The incidence of autocrime committed in the city division during the time of the campaign was compared with that in the preceding year. The incidence of burglary was then examined as a suitable indicator of the general pattern of crime in the area, and, as a further control, the pattern of autocrime in the campaign division was compared with that in two otherwise similar towns completely removed from the influence of the campaign.

In order to examine the possibility that there was either physical or temporal displacement of autocrime during the campaign period, a detailed analysis of crime complaint forms was necessary. To this end, information was extracted about the physical and temporal distribution of autocrime between September

---

[1] There are an estimated 60,000 vehicles registered in the city (Department of Environment statistics); the checks were carried out on weekday evenings in the high risk central area where publicity disseminated by police effort (as distinct from that of the media) was focussed, which comprised approximately one third of the city area. Given the relatively low vehicle ownership in this area, the number of cars owned by residents was probably well below a third of the city total (20,000), but the presence of additional cars whose owners were enjoying central entertainment facilities probably brought the estimated area total close to this figure.

1976 and February 1977, and compared with similar data extracted for offences committed during the campaign.

RESULTS

Security levels

There was no statistically significant change in the level of vehicle security recorded during the campaign. The security check made prior to the start of the campaign shows 19.0% of vehicles to be insecure—a proportion close to that revealed in previous security checks under similar conditions[1]—and checks during and after the campaign revealed levels of insecurity of 20.9%, 21.7% and 19.2%. In 51% of the cases of insecurity discovered, this was caused by an unlocked door, in 10% by an open window, and in 39% by an unlocked boot, or—in the case of estate cars—the tailgate to the vehicle; 17% of the insecure vehicles had more than one source of insecurity. The four checks were carried out under similar cold but dry conditions and the weather is unlikely to have prejudiced the results obtained.

These results suggest that the campaign had no measurable impact on the level of car security, and other data seem to support this inference. No relationship was found between insecurity levels and the parking location of vehicles, though the proximity of police posters in the central car parks would suggest that those parking there would be more likely to be aware of the campaign than other motorists. Furthermore, an analysis (carried out by using records held at Swansea to trace owners) of where the owners of the vehicles lived showed that those living within the campaign area were no more likely to have secured their vehicles than those from outside the city boundaries.

Autocrime statistics

No significant change in the level of autocrime was recorded either during or after the campaign. The total number of offences committed (195) during the campaign weeks represented a 38% increase on that recorded (141) for the corresponding weeks in the previous year; this pattern was also found in the control areas where autocrime increased 32% on the previous year's total. The difference between the campaign area and the two control towns in this respect was not statistically significant. Although the level of autocrime fell during the opening weeks of advertising, this downturn was in progress before the start of the exercise, and was not dissimilar from the pattern of burglary offences recorded at this time.

---

[1] In 1971, six urban forces carried out security checks in co-operation with 'Drive' magazine. The checks were carried out on Friday evenings in April and—across the forces—revealed a 22% level of insecurity (Automobile Association, 1971). It should be noted that the daytime level of insecurity is—for a variety of reasons—likely to be higher (Research Bureau Ltd., 1977).

A substantial part of the general rise in autocrime during the campaign was the result of a high level of 'taking' offences[1], these reached a peak during the final week of the campaign higher than any other weekly figure recorded during 1977. None of the weekly totals recorded, however, fell outside the range of normal fluctuations that would be expected for this crime.

There is evidence that during the campaign autocrime offences were more likely to be committed under cover of darkness than in daylight. Despite the difficulties of estimating when many offences occur[2], it is clear that—by comparison with the same weeks in the previous year—there was a statistically significant shift in the temporal distribution of these crimes during the campaign weeks ($p<.001$), to the effect that more offences were committed in the early hours of the morning (see Table 1.1).

Table 1:1

Autocrime: time of day at which offences occurred during the 5 campaign weeks and during the same 5 weeks in the previous year

Time period	Preceding year†	Campaign*
0600 – 1200	22.1%	7.3%
1200 – 1800	17.9%	11.2%
1800 – 2400	35.0%	32.0%
2400 – 0600	25.0%	49.5%

† 15 November to 20 December 1976
* 15 November to 20 December 1977

This change in the temporal distribution of crime may be attributed to the effect of the campaign itself, which could have persuaded offenders to act with more caution (cf. the response of car radio thieves to increased police activity reported in Parker, 1974) perhaps by fostering the expectation that the police were directing more attention to this form of criminality.

Alternatively, victims of autocrime aware of the publicity may have preferred to report that their vehicle had been stolen in the early hours of the morning, even if this was not so, rather than suffer the embarrassment of admitting that they had left their cars insecure or with expensive objects on display during the daytime. On the other hand, it is of course possible that the increase in offending during the campaign year led, at least in part, to the observed change in the temporal distribution of autocrime. It is conceivable that the higher proportion of crime committed between the hours of 2400 and 0600 was

[1] Police records maintain the distinction between the unauthorised taking and theft of vehicles, all offences being recorded in the latter category until such time as the vehicle is recovered. Because other forces make this distinction upon different criteria, and in many cases there is no doubt a failure to amend records to the effect that the vehicle in question has been recovered, these offences were treated as one.

[2] For the purpose of this comparison if the police or victim could not identify the exact time of the offence, this was treated as the mid-point between when the victim left the vehicle parked, and returned to discover that an offence had been committed.

9

accounted for, say, by the activities of a gang of youths (possibly from an outlying suburb) who might have begun to frequent the city in the evenings during the year of the campaign.

Other features of car crime seemed unaffected by the campaign. There was no evidence of the geographical displacement of offences outside the campaign area, nor did cars parked in different parking locations (such as streets, car parks, waste land etc.) become more or less vulnerable.

INTERPRETATION OF THE RESULTS

The findings of the present study are largely negative: first, during the campaign studied, police publicity proved to have no effect on drivers' locking behaviour; and second, its effect on autocrime was not to reduce it, but possibly to modify its form[1].

It would be simplistic to attribute evidence of the ineffectiveness of the campaign solely to the standard of its publicity. Set against the expenditure levels of larger commercial concerns, the direct costs incurred by the police in the conduct of these campaigns are low; but in this instance there is no reason to believe that by spending more on publicity the police could have achieved better results (though this possibility cannot be entirely ruled out). Small interview surveys[2] were carried out on two occasions during the campaign; both these surveys recorded encouraging levels of public awareness, established at 67% and 71% of all local drivers. This compares extremely favourably with the levels of awareness achieved in the 1976 national campaign (Research Bureau Ltd., 1977). Clearly a substantial number of car drivers do not comply with the advice given them by the police. This is generally construed by the police to be a sign of public complacency, but the explanation is probably more complex. This study, with others, provides evidence that not all insecurity arises from driver negligence; indeed, it suggests that drivers take into account a number of considerations when leaving their vehicles unlocked. It seems, for example, that the value of the vehicle driven may affect this judgement: evidence accrued in the experimental campaign shows that older vehicles are more likely to be left open. The perceived risk of theft over different lengths of time is doubtless another influence: several researchers (Bright, 1967; Research Bureau Ltd., 1977) have noted that drivers intending to leave their vehicles for long periods are more

---

[1] Though it was noted on page 6 that the principal cost of the campaign was that of police manpower, the question of cost effectiveness has not been closely examined. Nevertheless, the results of this research clearly suggest that little is to be gained from crime prevention officers conducting campaigns of this sort.

[2] These were carried out at random locations in the central shopping area. Having established that the respondent was a driver, the interviewer asked respondents whether they were aware the police were conducting a campaign, to describe the publicity material they had seen or heard (in order to distinguish the current impact from that of previous campaigns) and to state whether or not they lived in the city. Each survey covered 200 drivers, equally grouped by age and sex characteristics.

careful to secure them. Similarly, the increased probability of car windows being left open during hot weather (Research Bureau Ltd., 1977) is probably the result of drivers preferring to face the risk of theft rather than the discomfort of entering a hot vehicle.

Underlying these considerations is possibly the driver's judgement of whether locking will reduce the risk of car theft. Attitude research has borne out the view that many drivers, especially the young, are sceptical of the protection afforded by locking up their cars (Research Bureau Ltd., 1977). To some extent these drivers are correct in recognising that car locking does not totally remove the risk of theft. Parker's (1974) account of the activities of car radio thieves in Liverpool, for example, suggests that many offenders do not regard conventional locks as any impediment. Several police reports have illustrated this point more forcefully by examining the ways in which those apprehended for theft and unauthorised taking offences gained access to vehicles: for example, Hampshire Constabulary (1977) and Sunderland (Sunderland Crime Prevention Panel, 1975) have demonstrated the widespread use of duplicate keys as a means of gaining access to vehicles.

A more likely explanation for drivers' failure to lock their cars may be that they probably do not share the authorities' view of the seriousness of autocrime. It is likely that most drivers are aware that the risk of having their car stolen is low; even the owners of older vehicles probably appreciate this fact[1]. Many drivers may also believe that the loss of their car will generally constitute only a temporary inconvenience (72% of vehicles stolen during 1977 in the Metropolitan Police District, for example, were retrieved within 30 days), and that if this is not the case the loss will be borne by insurance. To the extent that car owners view autocrime from this perspective—and fail to consider the costs borne by the wider community in tracing and retrieving lost vehicles, or in paying increased insurance premiums—police appeals are unlikely to succeed.

IMPLICATIONS FOR CRIME PREVENTION

One important point to emerge from the various studies of autocrime is that it is not simply the 'professional' who will take a secure vehicle. Though it is conventional to distinguish the opportunist, or casual, thief from his professional counterpart, it is questionable whether there are many opportunists who will take a car simply because they notice one unlocked. It is probably more useful to distinguish three types of offender: those who will take a particular vehicle whether it is insecure or not (the professional falls in

---

[1] In the area of the experimental campaign, 85% of the theft and unauthorised taking offences recorded between September 1977 and February 1978 were directed at vehicles produced before 1971. If the life expectancy of these vehicles is set aside, and it is assumed that older vehicles throughout the country are equally as vulnerable, then the owners of such vehicles can expect to have their cars stolen once every 18 years (i.e. it can be calculated that during 1977 5.4% of the pre-1971 vehicles registered were subject to theft or unauthorised taking).

this category), those who will look for insecure vehicles, but break into a car if an unlocked vehicle is not found, and those who steal only unlocked vehicles. Various police reports show that the size of this latter group is often exaggerated; arguably, most autocrime offences are committed by fairly determined individuals who will not be deterred if they fail to find an unlocked vehicle. The fact that most thieves steal a car with a particular aim in mind (most frequently, as a means of transport, cf. McCaghy *et al*, 1977) would seem to support this view. So also does the fact that some makes of vehicle face an exaggerated risk of theft regardless of whether or not they are locked by their owners. Evidence from this study shows that although vehicles manufactured by Ford are less likely (given the numbers at risk) to be left insecure[1] than those of a number of other manufacturers, they are more likely to be subject to theft than others (see Table 1:2).

Common models of car appear generally to face exaggerated risks; it may be that these are attractive to thieves (particularly if fitted with comparatively unsophisticated door locks), but also these cars are less likely to attract police attention if stolen. Between September 1977 and February 1978, for example, the Ford Cortina accounted for 19.7% of all thefts in the study area.

Table 1:2
Proportion of vehicles subject to autocrime and proportion of vehicles found insecure, by make

Manufacturer	Autocrime	Insecurity
Ford	42.0%	20.9%
British Leyland	39.0%	47.0%
Chrysler	6.2%	9.4%
Vauxhall (GM)	5.9%	8.4%
Other British	4.1%	2.4%
Foreign	2.8%	11.9%
	100%	100%

NB: For various reasons, the figures in the columns of Table 1:2 are not directly comparable. The figures in the first column refer to all autocrime offences committed in the campaign division (between September 1977 and February 1978). In contrast the insecurity figures, which represent the cumulative total of all vehicles found insecure in the four campaign checks, refer to insecurity in a particular area and at a particular time. While these points cannot be ignored, it is unlikely that they can account for the differences observed in the levels of insecurity from one make of vehicle to the next; particularly since the sample of cars on which the insecurity figures were based was representative of vehicles in the campaign division.

---

[1] One explanation for this is that recent models of Ford have been fitted with 'automatic' boot locks (i.e. the catch can only be operated by key).

If most autocrime offences are committed by fairly determined individuals, there is little prospect that the police can reduce autocrime simply by persuading drivers to lock their vehicles. Those who do comply with police advice are likely to reduce their chances of having their car broken into or stolen[1]. But, given that a comparatively large pool of unprotected vehicles will remain even after the most forceful police compaign, it is likely that offenders will instead turn to these more vulnerable targets, and that overall levels of autocrime will probably remain unchanged. The probability that autocrime offences would be displaced in this manner has been argued by Riccio (1974) in the United States, and strong supportive evidence supplied by Mayhew et al (1976) who demonstrated that the effect of fitting steering column locks in this country has simply been to displace crime from protected vehicles (now an estimated 71% of the private cars and vans in Great Britain) to those unprotected.

Another drawback is that even in the unlikely event that the police achieved total compliance from the public (thus removing any risk of displacement) car thieves would probably respond by adopting more forceful means of entering vehicles and, again, any significant reduction in autocrime would be unlikely. Given the high proportion of offenders presently using duplicate keys as a means of entry to vehicles, the probability that others would operate in this way seems high. This itself is a problem amenable to technical solution, for more sophisticated door locks, which are not so simple to break, are available at relatively low cost (Birmingham Crime Prevention Panel, 1977). But, without legislative requirement, it would be necessary to gain manufacturers' approval, and whatever the means used, the police would continue to be faced with the task of persuading motorists to use the locking devices fitted to their cars.

One solution to the problem of displacement and the need to ensure public compliance has been the development of 'automatic' locking devices such as the steering column lock. Although not able to prevent offenders breaking into cars, devices of this type have proved an effective means of preventing the unauthorised theft of vehicles fitted with them, and—when all vehicles have been equipped as in West Germany in 1963 (Bundeskriminalamt, 1973)—this benefit has extended to reducing overall levels of unauthorised taking. In addition more sophisticated locking devices such as these do not appear to be so susceptible to changes in offenders' methods of operation, though there

---

[1] Baldwin (1974) has shown, from an examination of police crime records in Sheffield, that victims of autocrime offences were more likely to be careless in protecting their property than car drivers in general. Baldwin is, however, likely to have exaggerated the risk taken by those who fail to lock their vehicles. On the one hand his calculations were based on Bright's (1967) finding that 'typical' insecurity in Sheffield was of the order of 6% of vehicles, an improbably low estimate (see Introduction). On the other, his finding that about 34% of autocrime victims had left their vehicles insecure is much higher than the 16% found in a similar exercise in Plymouth prior to the campaign. Nonetheless, because many may be unwilling to admit leaving their vehicles insecure, both these figures probably constitute minimum estimates of victim liability.

have been some claims (e.g. Birmingham Crime Prevention Panel, 1977), as yet unsupported by firm evidence, that the initial impact of the steering column lock has diminished as ways of overcoming them become known[1]. There appear, therefore, to be some grounds for the optimism expressed in official circles that—though to date the level of unauthorised taking offences has not declined, and has instead been sustained by a dwindling pool of older, unprotected vehicles—as these vehicles are scrapped and replaced by vehicles fitted with steering locks so these offences will occur less frequently (cf. Mayhew et al, 1976).

SUMMARY

The study reported above examines the efficacy of police crime prevention publicity as a means of reducing autocrime. The campaign evaluated did not succeed in persuading a greater proportion of drivers to lock their cars, nor did the campaign effect a reduction in autocrime. It was argued that part of the reason for this public intransigence may be that many drivers do not perceive the risk and the consequences of having a car stolen as that serious.

While the individual driver who locks his car when leaving it unattended may reduce the risk of it being stolen, the conclusion is reached that publicity campaigns in any circumstances are unlikely to result in a noticeable reduction in the level of autocrime. Most autocrime offences are committed, not merely in response to the opportunity offered by an unlocked vehicle, but by more determined offenders. Thus even in the event of a campaign reducing the number of unlocked cars, offenders are likely to counteract this either by directing their attention to those vehicles left unlocked, or by changing their modes of operation.

---

[1] If this proves correct, it may become necessary to rely on some of the increasingly sophisticated devices available (like microprocessors) to protect new cars (see Ekblom (1979) for a discussion of such devices). For the present generation of vehicles, the solution may lie—insofar as 'breaking' is facilitated by lock wear—in including a check of the steering column lock among the requirements of the annual MOT check.

References

Automobile Association. 1971. 'When did you last see your car?' *Drive Magazine,* No. 18, Summer 1971.

Baldwin, J. 1974. 'The role of the victim in certain property offences'. *Criminal Law Review,* June, 353 – 358.

Birmingham Crime Prevention Panel. 1977. *How Safe is Your Car?* Working Party Report on Car Crime.

Bloom, D. & Twyman, T. 1978. 'The impact of economic change on the evaluation of advertising campaigns'. *Journal of the Market Research Society,* Vol. 2 No. 2.

Bright, J. A. 1967. *An Evaluation of Crime Cut Sheffield.* Police Research and Planning Branch Report No. 14/67 (official use only).

Bundeskriminalamt. 1973. Tagungsbericht der Arbeitstagung 'Kraftfahrzeug-diebstahl' beim Wiesbaden.

Caffyn, J. M. 1977. 'Measuring effects of advertising campaigns'. Paper given to the *12th Annual Conference of the Market Research Society.*

Clarke, R. V. G. & Cornish, D. B. 1972. *The Controlled Trial in Institutional Research—Paradigm or Pitfall for Penal Evaluators?* Home Office Research Study No. 15. London: HMSO.

Ekblom, P. J. 1979. 'A crime-free car?' *Research Bulletin No. 7,* 28 – 30. London: Home Office Research Unit.

Hampshire Constabulary. 1977. *Wheel Watch '77.* Crime Prevention Department.

Home Office. 1974. 'Nottinghamshire Constabulary Lock It (Vehicle Security Campaign)'. *Crime Prevention News,* No. 22.

Home Office. 1974. 'Southampton Car Security Week 1974'. *Crime Prevention News,* No. 24.

Home Office. 1975. 'Bath Car Campaign'. *Crime Prevention News,* Nos. 25 and 26.

Home Office. 1975. 'Short concentrated campaigns beat crime'. *Crime Prevention News,* No. 26.

Home Office. 1976. 'Road to riches'. *Crime Prevention News,* No. 32.

McCaghy, C. H., Giordano, P. C. & Henson, T. K. 1977. 'Auto theft – offender and offence characteristics'. *Criminology,* Vol. 15, No. 3.

Mayhew, P., Clarke, R. V. G., Sturman, A. & Hough, J. M. 1976. *Crime as Opportunity.* Home Office Research Study No. 34. London: HMSO.

Parker, H. J. 1974. *View from the Boys. A Sociology of Down-Town Adolescents.* Newton Abbot: David and Charles.

Research Bureau Limited. 1977. *Car Theft Campaign Evaluation 1976 – 77.* Prepared for Central Office of Information. Job No. 94066 – 11352.

Riccio, L. J. 1974. 'Direct deterrence—an analysis of the effectiveness of police patrol and other crime prevention technologies'. *Journal of Criminal Justice, 2.*

Sunderland Crime Prevention Panel. 1975. *Campaign to Reduce Thefts and Taking of Motor Vehicles Without the Owners' Consent.* Northumbria Police.

II Police Truancy Patrols

by Paul Ekblom

INTRODUCTION

Much research has shown that truants are particularly likely to come to the attention of the police for juvenile offences (Farrington, 1978; Tyerman, 1968; Tennent, 1971; Belson, 1975; May, 1975). Tennent, for example, showed that 25 – 40% of juvenile court defendants had truanted, but only 2 – 20% of the total school population. Farrington, studying both teacher-rated and self-reported truants in secondary schools, found that roughly half were delinquents compared with some 15% of the remaining children.

Tyerman (1968) has argued that if a pupil finds he can successfully avoid school, it may be a step to believing that he can just as easily defy authority in other ways. Cohen (1955) is of the opinion that anti-social attitudes are engendered by truancy to the extent that this combines with school failure. Equally likely, though, is the possibility that truancy leads to delinquency by virtue of the greater opportunities the truant would seem to have for getting into trouble (cf. Mannheim, 1965).

Whatever the link between delinquency and truancy, the level of truancy in this country causes concern. Statistics pertaining to truancy[1] which derive from attendance records have several limitations (cf. Williams, 1974), but calculating from a school age population of 11 million (Annual Abstract of Statistics, 1977), upwards of a quarter of a million children probably truant on any one day in Great Britain.

POLICE TRUANCY PATROLS

The police endorse the belief that truants are more likely than other children to become delinquent. Furthermore, while some officers in the Metropolitan Police District who have been involved in running truancy patrols now argue that truants avoid offending at times when they would be conspicuous (a view supported by Belson's (1975) self-report study but countered by the present Commissioner (McNee, 1979)), most forces believe that much daytime crime is committed by children who should be in school. In any event, some seven or eight forces in Britain have recently established projects aimed at reducing truancy, the majority of which are special patrols. Apart from patrols which were operated until 1975 in a number of MPD divisions (Devlin, 1974; *Times Educational Supplement*, 18 January 1974), patrols have operated in Gloucestershire, South Wales, Sussex, Avon and Somerset, Northamptonshire, and in a sub-division of the Glasgow force (Haining, 1973).

The more formal patrols have consisted of one or two officers, frequently accompanied by, or co-operating with, education welfare officers (EWOs),

---

[1] Truancy is taken here to mean illegitimate absence from school with or without the knowledge and connivance of parents; it is calculated as the proportion of days lost out of the total possible number of days' attendance at school.

and have covered a sub-division, or an area around a large comprehensive school. Unaccompanied children encountered on the streets during school hours are challenged and, if no plausible excuse is presented, are often returned directly to school. Follow-up visits by EWOs are frequently made to the parents of the children deemed to be truanting.

Records have usually been kept of the numbers of children stopped, and occasionally attempts have been made to see whether local crime has fallen during patrol periods. For many patrols for which data are available (not all are adequately documented), large numbers of children were picked up—for example 200 a day in Hackney, mostly aged 13 – 14. Comparing crime figures during patrol periods with those of the previous year, a 12-day sweep in Brixton and Lambeth, for example, was said to result in autocrime falling by 26% and petty crime by 30%. In Glasgow, during an unusually long patrol of 10 weeks, 53 crimes attributed to juveniles were reported as having been committed during school hours, with 56 apprehensions of juveniles; in the same period the previous year, 115 crimes were reported as committed during school hours, for which 22 children were apprehended. As far as can be judged from school registration figures, the Glasgow patrol seemed to have considerably improved the attendance of persistent as well as casual truants.[1].

Whilst previous assessments of truancy patrols have focussed largely on police crime figures, there is a strong case to be made that these are inadequate (even, as in Glasgow, when used in combination with school registration figures). First, crimes known to the police may be neither representative of, nor bear a constant relationship with, the actual level of crime. Second, the use of the previous year's statistics as a comparison figure is less than ideal since the weather, the position of holidays, etc., may vary. Third, police figures do not in most cases show who committed an offence (i.e. child or adult), or its exact timing (i.e. in or out of school hours). Related to this is the uncertainty as to whether offences prevented during school hours by patrols have merely been 'displaced' to other times or places. Finally, whilst the percentage falls in crime seem large the absolute numbers are often small and thus unreliable.

The study reported below was an attempt both to evaluate the need for truancy patrols and their effectiveness in reducing the level of daytime crime by truants. It was judged necessary to examine a patrol set up experimentally rather than to examine one retrospectively, using information additional to that provided by the police. The help was sought of the Avon and Somerset Constabulary, because it had prior experience of truancy patrols and because Bristol was judged fairly representative of a number of moderately urbanised regions in which patrols have been run.

---

[1] Two truancy patrols conducted in California are discussed by White *et al.* (1975). One two-week patrol in San Bernardino involving nine police officers appeared to reduce daytime burglaries, though from the data given it is not clear whether this was a chance effect. A four-week patrol in Glendale coincided with a somewhat more definite fall in daylight burglaries.

METHOD OF EVALUATION

Design

The study comprised two time series of observations, before and after half-term in the Spring term of 1978 (see Figure 1). In each half of the term, observations (comprising various daily counts of children at large during school hours) were taken before, during and after a week's patrolling; these were then considered in relation to a number of crime indices.

FIG. 1: The Design

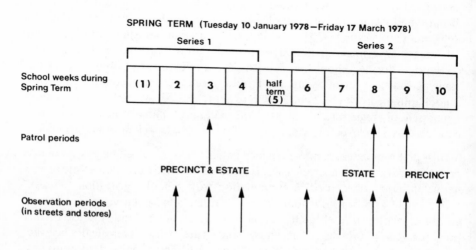

Patrols and observations were conducted in two city divisions—the central shopping precinct and an outlying council estate. To check for displacement the patrols in the second series were staggered such that the patrol in the precinct occurred a week later than that in the estate. In the opinion of the police the precinct was the most likely destination of those displaced from the estate.

The amount of truancy patrolling over the school term (four patrol weeks in all) was greater than that usually provided by the police in the area (two days per term). This reflected a pragmatic decision to seek effects of measurable strength whilst not exceeding by too great a margin the level of resources the police feel able to devote to this activity on a regular basis. (It was judged rather unrealistic in this respect to evaluate a patrol of the length adopted in Glasgow.) Publicity and teacher co-operation (common features of truancy initiatives) were avoided to single out the effect of special police presence. The method of patrolling was typical: a group comprising a male and female police constable (both uniformed) and an EWO covered a given area, interviewing children without adults, and where necessary returning them home or to school. The precinct team worked on foot; the estate team mostly in marked cars.

Several confounding events imposed themselves upon the study, most significant of all being the closure due to snow of all the schools in Bristol for at least one day during week 7 (when it was originally intended that the estate patrol would take place). This resulted in the estate and precinct patrols being shifted to the weeks shown in Figure 1, cutting short the post-patrol measurement period and reducing the quality of the week-to-week comparisons.

Data recorded

i. *Police patrol figures*
Patrols were asked to record the age and sex of children stopped, the time any action was taken and their judgement of the validity of any excuses proffered. Unfortunately, a misunderstanding resulted so that in many cases the author had to make the latter judgement himself on the basis of the police description of the excuses given.

ii. *School registration figures*
For each week of the Spring term, the number of absences (for whatever cause) was found for the boys' and girls' comprehensive schools in the estate (there were no schools in the precinct area). This was partly to see whether patrols were directly affecting attendance levels. It was also meant as a way of establishing whether background variations in absence, occurring independently of any patrol effects, might be affecting the principal dependent variable, namely the numbers of children counted on the streets. For this latter purpose it was also necessary to take note of absence figures from two schools similar to those in the estate, situated in a district that was comparable to, but well removed from, the patrol areas.

iii. *Child counts on the street*
Research workers also made counts each day, on regular routes and times, of school age children seen at large between 10 a.m. – 12 noon and 2 p.m. – 3.30 p.m., who were not obviously on any school activity. For each child details were noted of sex, approximate age and whether he/she was alone, with other children, or with adults. Each morning and afternoon two researchers spent some half an hour together driving round the streets of the estate and walking round the shopping centre there; 30 minutes were also passed walking round the precinct. In the estate only one researcher counted; in the precinct both researchers counted whilst following separate routes. No child was approached by the researchers and assumptions were made about the proportion of children counted who had legitimate reasons for being out of school. In all cases the *change* in numbers from week to week was of central interest, rather

21

than the absolute totals counted, since these could depend on arbitrary factors, not least the possibility of some double-counting of children by the two researchers in the precinct. An attempt to allow for this in the analysis of statistical significance is noted in Table 2:2.

iv. *Child counts in a department store*

It was thought possible that truants might attempt to avoid the patrols by going into large stores in the city centre. By arrangement with the management of a large department store in the precinct therefore, the two researchers spent a further 30 minutes each morning and each afternoon counting as inconspicuously as possible the children who entered the store. By judicious positioning most of the main entrances were covered.

v. *Store detectives' records*

Since, according to some sources, shoplifting is the offence most frequently committed by truants, it was arranged that store detectives from about ten large stores in the precinct would keep records of shoplifting by children in school hours. In the event, however, so few kept up their initial enthusiasm that the figures were considered unreliable.

vi. *Police daily crime reports*

Weekly totals were derived of offences reported as taking place within each patrol boundary[1], which *could* have been committed in school hours (not all offences could be precisely located in time) and which by their nature *could* have been committed by children (offences such as cheque frauds, or those where adult suspects were described, were eliminated from the total).

vii. *Juvenile bureau entries*

Since offences which are followed by immediate arrest if they are detected (such as shoplifting) do not appear in daily crime reports, to avoid missing these the weekly totals of all entries in the juvenile bureau records were derived for the respective divisions in which the patrols were located.

RESULTS

Patrol figures

In the first half of the term the patrol in the precinct picked up 32 children virtually all with unacceptable excuses. (For this patrol particularly, it is not known whether the patrol recorded every child approached.) The estate patrol recorded 136, of whom 46 (34%) had excuses judged unacceptable by the author.

---

[1] This is seen as justified in the light of a study by Baldwin *et al.* (1976), where the majority of offences by children under 16 appeared to have been committed within a mile of home (Table 12, p. 83).

In the second half of term the precinct patrol picked up 29 children, only 8 (28%) of whom had poor excuses (again judged by the author); the estate patrol interviewed 127, of whom 53 (42%) had poor excuses. The discrepancies in the numbers of children picked up in the two areas (which hold up even when differences between the street count figures from both areas are taken into account) are interesting since they may imply that patrols catch children more easily in the suburbs by car than in the central area on foot. The fact that transporting children to an outlying school took up more time in the precinct than the purely local requirements in the estate could not be considered responsible for the observed differences, because not a great number of children were taken back to school in either division. It seems more likely that children could readily spot the foot patrol and more easily elude them.

School registration figures

An average of 476 children were officially absent from the comprehensive schools in the estate at each registration, of whom national estimates would conservatively suggest that some 100 were truanting. While these figures cannot be meaningfully compared with the street count data, they are useful in assessing the impact of patrols. The average daily number of children of appropriate age and with poor excuses, who were picked up by the estate patrols was 8—a small proportion, that is, of those at whom the patrols were aimed.

Counts of children

The average daily counts of children without adults were 27 in the precinct, 15 in the store and 26 in the estate. Some of these children are likely to have had legitimate grounds for being out of school, but probably not in so high a proportion as that reported by the patrols (some two-thirds), since it is reasonable to expect that children illegitimately at large would have sought more than their fellows to avoid the police. The corresponding figures for children seen in the three locations *with* adults were 28, 12 and 12 and it is possible that a fair proportion of these, too, were truanting or feigning sickness with the condonement or assistance of their parents[1]. The child counts[2] are presented in weekly totals in Table 2:1. Certain corrections which have been made to the figures are explained in the Appendix, which also describes checks on their reliability.

---

[1] In the recent Hastings patrols, roughly half the children recorded as truants had their absence judged as 'condoned by parents'.

[2] Unless otherwise stated the counts refer to children observed alone or in groups without adults, for whom there was considered by the researchers to be no doubt as to whether they were of compulsory school age.

Table 2:1

Corrected weekly totals of child counts

Week	Precinct	Store	Estate	Event
2	174	105	110	—
3	144	93	130	estate and precinct patrol
4	128	56	117	—
5				half-term
6	185	73	150	—
7	164	95	296	snow closure
8	124	60	101	estate patrol
9	78	26	91	precinct patrol
10	94	20	69	—

It would appear at first sight from Table 2:1 that the patrolling resulted in sizeable falls in the numbers of children counted. (Percentage falls are presented in Table 2:2).

Table 2:2

Percentage falls in child counts between the week preceding and the week(s) after the patrol periods

Series 1		% fall	Series 2		% fall
Precinct	wks 2 – 4	26	Precinct	wks 8 – 10	24*
Store	wks 2 – 4	47†	Store	wks 8 – 10	67†
Estate	wks 2 – 4	4	Estate	wks 6 – 9	39†
			Estate	wks 6 – 10	54†

* denotes p < .05;   † p < .001 (Chi-squared)

NB: Week 7 is omitted from all comparisons; the child count scores in the precinct were reduced by one-third when calculating Chi-squared values to correct for possible double-counting.

Significant or near-significant drops occurred in the precinct and the store before half-term (series 1) and in all three locations after half-term (series 2). This most favourable interpretation of the results is further enhanced by the apparent lack of displacement of children in week 8 from the estate to the precinct, although outside events reduced the quality of the test. Similarly there is no indication of displacement from the streets of the precinct to stores, either from the store counts or from store detectives' records (whatever their faults), which showed no rise in shoplifting by children during or after patrols.

There are, however, several good reasons for attributing a large proportion of the observed changes to background influences rather than to the patrols[1].

---

[1] There were no significant differences for any of the observations (patrol figures, child counts, store detectives' records) as a function of day-to-day changes in rainfall. Breakdown of the observations by sex, by age and by children in groups and alone revealed few consistent differences from the overall trends.

i. More children were picked up by the patrols in the estate, yet the falls appeared stronger in the precinct and the store; the falls were greatest in the store, where the patrols rarely went[1].

ii. The falls in the second series—where the pre-patrol measurement period was longer—appeared to begin immediately after half-term, before the patrols operated. It is unfortunate, however, that the numbers in the precinct and the store in week 6 may have been increased to some extent by private school holidays.

iii. In the estate (in series 2) the observed falls were greater in magnitude in the second week after the patrol. Whilst it is reasonable to expect a fall in children on the streets the week after patrolling, any further drop is difficult to put down to police action; moreover, the falls in the previous weeks also become suspect.

iv. Over the whole term, the absence figures for the schools in the estate tended to mirror those for the control schools outside it. This indicates that a fair proportion of the variance in attendance at the former schools was probably due to extraneous factors. In the second series, the child counts in all locations also tended to follow the same pattern as absence figures in the control schools[2], though the correlations were not large enough to suggest that all the changes in the child counts can be explained as background rather than patrol effects. (In the first series, the weekly changes in street counts *opposed* the pattern of control absences.)

v. Much the strongest evidence arguing against attributing the observed falls to the patrols comes from an examination of the *daily* changes in street counts. In the precinct in the first series, and in all locations in the second, much of the drop occurring in each patrol week took place on the Monday, when patrols would be expected to have least effect. This was generally the reverse of the patterns observed in pre-patrol weeks, where Mondays tended to yield the highest counts of children.

All in all, the child counts when taken in context strongly suggest that background factors played a greater part in determining the numbers of children visible than did the patrols—although it is clearly not possible to provide firmer evidence of their relative influences.

Store detectives' records

Over the eight school weeks of the study period, some nine store detectives in five stores saw only ten definite cases of shoplifting by children in school hours, and 60 suspected cases (many of which may have been unsupported by any concrete observations). The corresponding figures taken separately from the store where researchers counted children (whose detectives maintained

---

[1] It is unlikely that the falls were the result of the observers' presence since the drop took two weeks from the start of counting in series 1, but four weeks in series 2.

[2] There are positive but not quite significant rank correlations between them, ranging from precinct male $\times$ control male tau $= +.7$, to estate female $\times$ control female tau $= +.3$.

good records throughout the study) are one definite case and 13 suspected. An estimated total of some 2600 children[1] entered this store during school hours over the eight-week period, giving a minimum proportion of 1/186 of these children being probable shoplifters who were sighted by store detectives. The number who were shoplifting but who were not spotted remains unknown but, as the children themselves were probably aware, the store detectives paid them special attention if they entered during school hours (cf. May, 1978).

Daily crime reports and juvenile bureau entries

Combining the patrol areas' scores for precinct and estate in the first series resulted in weekly crime totals of 13, 9 (the week when the patrols operated) and 14—a statistically insignificant fall in the patrol week. The figures from the second series are even less clearcut. There were no significant differences to these patterns when various offences were considered separately—no evidence, that is, that street crimes (e.g. car theft) fell as a result of patrols whilst off-street crimes (e.g. burglary) rose.

As regards the juvenile bureau entries, in neither series and in neither division is there any evidence to suggest that patrols reduced crime—indeed in the precinct the number of entries rose throughout the first series.

CONCLUSIONS

The effectiveness of patrols

It is not easy to draw clearcut conclusions from this research. The results were obscured by an unexpectedly low rate of daytime offending by truants, and by unkind background variations and coincident events. These included the fact that the counts of children in the streets and the store in the week after half term were probably inflated by children legitimately away from private schools, and—more important—that all the Bristol schools were closed for part of one week due to snow. However, the results make it hard to attribute much of the observed falls in the numbers of children on the streets and in the store to the activity of the Bristol patrols. The most generous assessment possible is that the patrols may have played a small contributory part, lasting up to two weeks after each single week of patrolling.

Clearly, the patrols may have influenced the behaviour of some children, if only those picked up and found to have poor excuses for being absent from school. The present study cannot show whether the attendance of these children subsequently improved (as was claimed in Glasgow), or indeed whether the patrols caused any *other* children to return to school or perhaps stay inside their homes. The lack of any clear effect of the patrol may be because the patrols posed little threat to truants; this is strongly suggested by the likelihood that only a small proportion of truants at large were stopped.

---

[1] This figure in fact refers to the number of entries made by children. Some children may have entered the store more than once.

In terms of the consequences for a child of being picked up, his or her experience at the hands of the patrol is unlikely to be unpleasant in itself (for first-timers, fear of the unknown perhaps being more aversive than the real thing); and further action by the school or by EWOs in follow-up visits may or may not constitute a threat.

The extent to which children in the relevant area became aware of patrolling is unknown; it is of course possible that a patrol run on a routine basis (and accompanied by more publicity, a point returned to later) could deter more children from truancy than the practice adopted for the present study; alternatively, truants could become more familiar with the threat, and more skilled at, or concerned with, escaping apprehension. Issues such as the extent of deterrence achieved or the degree of awareness of patrols might have been clarified by interviewing children in the patrol areas, but this was judged impractical on several grounds, not least of which was resources. It was also felt that interviewing during the study period might have interfered with the effects of patrols, while retrospective interviews (of necessity carried out after the three-week Easter break) would have overtaxed the memory (if not the imagination) of the children concerned.

In relation to the effect of patrols on crime, the child count had been intended to serve as a sensitive but indirect indicator relating to the *opportunity* of children to offend. As the fall in numbers of children observed can at best be attributed only in a small degree to the patrols, it cannot be concluded that these would have been responsible for a reduction in crime as a result of fewer children being at large. In fact, there was no direct evidence from police or store detectives' records that crime went down during or after the patrolling period, though there is a small possibility that some fall in crime *not* reflected in the records examined resulted from the fact that fewer numbers of children were to be seen.

Advice to the police
Advice to the police on the effectiveness of truancy patrols in achieving immediate cuts in crime cannot, however, consist of a categorical rejection generalised from the Bristol experience. Though it is difficult to assess how rigorous the evaluations of patrols conducted by other forces were, it has been claimed that they were more successful. If their evaluations can be relied upon, the relatively strong effects on numbers of children who truanted and committed offences during school hours reported by the Glasgow and the several London patrols may be attributed to a number of factors. Differing circumstances (e.g. higher child density) may have been responsible, together with longer patrol periods and greater publicity for the projects. It may also have been possible that any publicity given, or any involvement of school staff in providing records of truants' attendance (neither of which occurred in the present study), may have led teachers and parents to make greater efforts to keep children in school. This would have given a false picture of the effectiveness of patrolling.

Each police force must of course make its own decision concerning truancy patrols, based on knowledge of local conditions. One important fact that emerged during the study was the apparently diminutive size of the problem posed by truants in Bristol. In the estate area there were, as mentioned before, some 500 absences at each registration in the two comprehensive schools and perhaps 100 truants among them. Yet it emerged during the study that *only half a dozen crimes were reported per week which might, or might not, have been committed by children in school time.* Admittedly, the majority of petty offences are probably not reported to the police but even allowing for this there would appear to be little reason for the police (in Bristol, at least) to devote special attention to truants with a view to achieving immediate and significant cuts in crime. The amount of school-time shoplifting by children in the city centre (a statistic that merits separate scrutiny) would equally seem to constitute no major source of trouble, *with some ten children recorded as offending in five major stores over eight weeks.* All this underlines the general need for the police (and the various bodies which seek to influence their activities) to assess carefully the case for committing special resources to deal with a perceived problem: as Belson (1975) found, truants probably tend to break the law outside school hours, which runs counter to the conventional police wisdom.

If a police force has judged crime committed by truants to be worthy of special action it is important that any trial innovation includes some means of evaluating its effectiveness. (Outside research staff cannot of course be relied on to investigate each diverse case.) For truancy patrols it is still felt that counts of children on the street (conducted by plain clothes officers other than those concerned with the patrols—possibly by cadets) are perhaps the best index of the effect of patrolling, being more sensitive indicators than police crime figures, and enabling the influence of background factors to be taken more easily into account.

On the evidence of this study it seems that for truancy patrols to be effective they may require more resources than many forces are willing or able to provide; certainly a week's patrolling does not seem adequate. In the current situation of financial stringency this further augments the need to see whether action against truants is warranted and whether any truancy patrol that is conducted is effective.

With this caution in mind, the present study can offer some guidance to police forces who consider that their local circumstances merit the operation of truancy patrols. Foot patrols may be more effective in central shopping areas, car patrols in suburbs. The wearing of uniforms on patrol appears to have advantages in all contexts. Although easier for children to spot, they may serve to emphasise the presence of the police and allay fears the public could have on seeing strangers leading off children. (It is fair to note, though, that where plain clothes have been worn on truancy patrols no problems have arisen.) The extent to which truancy work is popular with the police officers taking part

28

remains unclear, but it is probable that officers who have had some experience in juvenile liaison work would be more willing and better able to carry out the duties.

Also, truancy patrols almost certainly benefit from the involvement of EWOs. The legal basis for apprehending children and conducting them back home or to school remains somewhat vague, but the position of patrols operating without EWOs seems legally weaker[1]. These are, moreover, less likely to be effective both in assessing the excuses of children encountered, and in keeping the returned children in school on a long-term basis. Whilst the patrols whose activities have been reported seem to have given rise to little in the way of complaints by children, school staff or parents (indeed, most parents seem to have been grateful for the action taken), it is felt that the presence of an EWO in or working closely with[2] the patrol team is useful at least until the police officers involved have gained experience of situations which require considerable tact and skill.

Patrols in a wider context

Relevant to the police decision of whether or not to conduct patrols are a number of issues additional to the central one of achieving an immediate cut in daytime crime by truants. For one thing, it might be argued that the officers engaged on truancy patrol duty are just as effective in deterring adults from crime as they might be when patrolling the streets on normal beat duty. Another advantage that has figured in several of the police reports on patrols is that they pick up absconders from various juvenile institutions. In relation to truants themselves, patrolling may serve to reduce crime in that a child's truancy, offending and associated social problems come earlier to the attention of parents, school and social workers. While some patrols have been established with this longer-term objective in view, the present study can throw little light on it. Additionally, while under some circumstances truancy patrols may be counter-productive (they may dramatise truancy, or if clumsily conducted antagonise truants further), it is equally likely that they can serve to increase general police-pupil-teacher contacts, in line with the aims of the police juvenile liaison bureaux established over the past few years. From a public relations point of view, truancy patrolling on an occasional basis may yet be valuable to the police as an exercise to show the community their involvement in alleviating the problems posed by juveniles.

---

[1] The Metropolitan Police when operating truancy patrols relied on Section 28 of the Children and Young Persons Act 1969, which empowers a constable to take to a place of safety a child who appears to be at risk in a number of defined ways. It was subsequently established, it seems, that Section 28 did not cover truanting children and patrols were therefore stopped in 1975. Other forces, however, have not made this interpretation; further, the EWOs with whom they co-operate have the power of *loco parentis* vested in the local education authority.

[2] In some patrols operated by other forces the EWO was based at a local police station and dealt with children as the police brought them in.

If suitably lengthy patrols do manage to keep children in school, they may have educational benefits additional to crime preventive ones. Again, it must be noted that the present study has done little to evaluate these. Some patrols (Glasgow and Sussex, for example) have been run, however, at least partly with educational goals in mind.

To conclude, it remains a moot point how much use truancy patrols can be unless accompanied by an increased parental interest in and commitment to their children's attendance at school. Relevant to this was the noticeable presence in Bristol during the study of school age children out shopping with their parents in school hours. The greater effectiveness of truancy patrols may sometimes also require improvements in the security routines in the schools themselves—tighter registration procedures, spot checks, monitoring of exits and so forth (cf. Boyson, 1974). In the current study, for example, two girls were able to play truant again not long after being taken back there by the estate patrol. It should also be borne in mind, however, that although short-term tactical measures (such as truancy patrols) may be of value in some circumstances, many educationalists and others would argue[1] that it is even more important to consider whether the goal of producing educated, relatively law-abiding citizens may ultimately best be served by capturing the interest and motivation of children, rather than simply by capturing their persons.

---

[1] Some useful discussions of the relationship between truancy and educational processes may be found in Tyerman, 1968; Turner, 1974; and Carroll, 1978.

Appendix

Corrections to, and reliability checks on the child counts

Some sort of representative figure for the week in which schools were closed down for one day because of snow was obtained by multiplying the sum of the days on which schools were open by 5/4. This still probably gives an inflated figure and as a consequence week 6 was preferred as the comparison pre-patrol week for the estate in series 2.

Figures for the last week (in all three locations) were amended by subtracting the last day's scores (which were high due to the end of term) and multiplying by 5/4. Although this may have removed a Friday peak (which appeared only infrequently in the study), the somewhat swollen figures for the last Thursday suffice to remedy this.

A number of different observers assisted the author for about a week each. As a check on inter-observer reliability, counts in the precinct by the author and the other researchers grouped together were compared for 20 randomly-selected days from both series. The only significant difference was that the author recorded fewer numbers of children under 10.

Eight immediate re-counts were conducted at various random days in the second series (a repeat of the drive round the estate), yielding a significant test-retest correlation of $r = +.73$.

References

Baldwin, J., Bottoms, A. E. & Walker, M. A. 1976. *The Urban Criminal.* London: Tavistock.

Belson, W. A. 1975. *Juvenile Theft: the Causal Factors.* London: Harper and Row.

Boyson, R. 1974. 'The need for realism'. In Turner, B. (Ed.), *Truancy.* London: Ward Lock.

Carroll, H. C. M. (Ed.). 1977. *Absenteeism in South Wales.* University College Swansea: Faculty of Education.

Cohen, A. K. 1955. *Delinquent Boys: the Culture of the Gang.* Glencoe, Ill.: The Free Press.

Devlin, T. 1974. 'Truants who are pushing up London's crime rate'. *The Times,* 28 June.

Farrington, D. P. (forthcoming) 'Truancy, delinquency, the home and the school'. In Hersov, L. & Berg, I. (Eds.), *Problems of School Attendance —School Refusal and Truancy.* London: Wiley.

Haining, Supt. W. 1973. 'Glasgow's truancy patrol, 24 April – 28June 1973'. *Police Review,* 81/4219, 1629.

Mannheim, H. 1965. *Comparative Criminology.* London: Routledge and Kegan Paul.

May, D. 1975. 'Truancy, school absenteeism and delinquency'. *Scottish Educational Studies, 7,* 97 – 107.

May, D. 1978. 'Juvenile shoplifters and the organisation of store security: a case study in the social construction of delinquency'. *International Journal of Criminology and Penology, 6,* 137 – 160.

McNee, Sir D. 1979. 'Crime and the young'. *Police Journal, 52,* 5 – 14.

Tennent, T. G. 1971. 'School non-attendance and delinquency'. *Educational Research, 13,* 185 – 190.

Times Educational Supplement. 1974. 'DES seek the facts on truants'. 18 January.

Turner, B. (Ed.). 1974. *Truancy.* London: Ward Lock.

Tyerman, M. J. 1968. *Truancy*. London: University of London Press.

White, T. W., Regan, K. J., Waller, J. D. & Wholey, J. S. 1975. *Police Burglary Preventive Programs (Prescriptive Package)*. National Institute of Law Enforcement and Criminal Justice, Law Enforcement Assistance Administration, US Department of Justice. Washington DC: Government Printing Office.

Williams, P. 1974. 'Collecting the figures'. In Turner, B. (Ed.), *Truancy*. London: Ward Lock.

Publications

Titles already published for the Home Office

Postage extra

Studies in the Causes of Delinquency and the Treatment of Offenders

1. Prediction methods in relation to borstal training. Hermann Mannheim and Leslie T. Wilkins. 1955. vi + 276pp. (11 340051 9) £3.

2. †Time spent awaiting trial. Evelyn Gibson. 1960. 46pp. (34-368-2) 27p.

3. †Delinquent generations. Leslie T. Wilkins. 1960. 20pp. (11 340053 5) 16p.

4. Murder. Evelyn Gibson and S. Klein. 1961. 44pp. (11 340054 3) 30p.

5. Persistent criminals. A study of all offenders liable to preventive detention in 1956. W. H. Hammond and Edna Chayen. 1963. x + 238pp. (34-368-5) £1.25.

6. Some statistical and other numerical techniques for classifying individuals. P. McNaughton-Smith. 1965. 34pp. (34-368-6) 17½p.

7. Probation research: a preliminary report. Part I. General outline of research. Part II. Study of Middlesex probation area (SOMPA). Steven Folkard Kate Lyon, Margaret M. Carver, Erica O'Leary. 1966. vi + 58pp. (11 340374 7) 42p.

8. *Probation research: national study of probation. Trends and regional comparisons in probation (England and Wales). Hugh Barr and Erica O'Leary. 1966. viii + 52pp. (34-368-8) 25p.

9. *Probation research. A survey of group work in the probation service. Hugh Barr. 1966. viii + 96pp. (34-368-9) 40p.

10. *Types of delinquency and home background. A validation study of Hewitt and Jenkins' hypothesis. Elizabeth Field. 1967. vi + 22pp. (34-368-10) 14p.

11. *Studies of female offenders. No. 1—Girls of 16 – 20 years sentenced to borstal or detention centre training in 1963. No. 2—Women offenders in the Metropolitan Police District in March and April 1957. No. 3—A description of women in prison on January 1. 1965. Nancy Goodman and Jean Price. 1967. vi + 78pp. (34-368-11) 30p.

12. *The use of the Jesness Inventory on a sample of British probationers. Martin Davies. 1967. iv + 20pp. (34-368-12) 11p.

13. The Jesness Inventory: application to approved school boys. Joy Mott. 1969. iv + 28pp. (11 340063 2) 17½p.

Home Office Research Studies

1. Workloads in children's departments. Eleanor Grey. 1969. vi + 75pp. (11 340101 9) 37½p.

2. Probationers in their social environment. A study of male probationers aged 17 – 20, together with an analysis of those reconvicted within twelve months. Martin Davies. 1969. vii + 204pp. (11 340102 7) 87½p.

*Copies available from Home Office Research Unit, (Information Section), 50 Queen Anne's Gate, London SW1.

†Out of print. Photostat copies can be purchased from Her Majesty's Stationery Office upon request.

3. Murder 1957 to 1968. A Home Office Statistical Division report on murder in England and Wales. Evelyn Gibson and S. Klein (with annex by the Scottish Home and Health Department on murder in Scotland) 1969. vi + 94pp. (11 340103 5) 60p.

4. Firearms in crime. A Home Office Statistical Division report on indictable offences involving firearms in England and Wales. A. D. Weatherhead and B. M. Robinson. 1970. viii + 37pp. (11 340104 3) 30p.

5. †Financial penalties and probation. Martin Davies. 1970. vii + 38pp. (11 340105 1) 30p.

6. Hostels for probationers. Study of the aims, working and variations in the effectiveness of male probation hostels with special reference to the influence of the environment on delinquency. Ian Sinclair. 1971. iv + 199pp. (11 340106 X) £1.15.

7. Prediction methods in criminology including a prediction study of young men on probation. Frances H. Simon. 1971. xi + 233pp. (11 340107 8) £1.25.

8. †Study of the juvenile liaison scheme in West Ham 1961 – 1965. Marilyn Taylor. 1971. vi + 45pp. (11 340108 6) 35p.

9. Explorations in after-care. I—After-care units in London, Liverpool and Manchester. Martin Silberman (Royal London Prisoners' Aid Society), Brenda Chapman. II—After-care hostels receiving a Home Office grant. Ian Sinclair and David Snow (HORU). III—St Martin of Tours House, Aryeh Leissner (National Bureau for Co-operation in Child Care). 1971. xi + 168pp. (11 340102 4) 85p.

10. A survey of adoption in Great Britain. Eleanor Grey in collaboration with R. M. Blunden. 1971. ix + 168pp. (11 340110 8) 95p.

11. †Thirteen-year-old approved school boys in 1962. Elizabeth Field, W. H. Hammond and J. Tizard. 1971. ix + 45pp. (11 340111 6) 35p.

12. Absconding from approved schools. R. V. G. Clarke and D. N. Martin. 1971. vi + 145pp. (11 340112 4) 85p.

13. An experiment in personality assessment of young men remanded in custody. H. Sylvia Anthony. 1972. viii + 79pp. (11 340113 2) 52½p.

14. Girl offenders aged 17 – 20 years. I—Statistics relating to girl offenders aged 17 – 20 years from 1960 to 1970. II—Re-offending by girls released from borstal or detention centre training. III—The problems of girls released from borstal training during their period on after-care. Jean Davies and Nancy Goodman. 1972. v + 77pp. (11 340114 0) 52½p.

15. The controlled trial in institutional research—paradigm or pitfall for penal evaluators? R. V. G. Clarke and D. B. Cornish. 1972. v + 33pp. (11 340115 9) 29p.

16. A survey of fine enforcement. Paul Softley. 1973. v + 65pp. (11 340116 7) 47p.

17. An index of social environment designed for use in social work research. Martin Davies. 1973. v + 61pp. (11 340117 5) 47p.

18. Social enquiry reports and the probation service. Martin Davies and Andrea Knopf. 1973. v + 47pp. (11 340118 3) 50p.

19. Depression, psychopathic personality and attempted suicide in a borstal sample. H. Sylvia Anthony. 1973. viii + 44pp. (0 11 340119 1) 36½p.

20. The use of bail and custody by London magistrates' courts before and after the Criminal Justice Act 1976. Frances Simon and Mollie Weatheritt. 1974. vi + 78pp. (0 11 340120 5) 57p.

21. Social work in the environment. A study of one aspect of probation practice. Martin Davies, with Margaret Rayfield, Alaster Calder and Tony Fowles. 1974. x + 164pp. (0 11 340121 3) £1.10.

22. Social work in prisons. An experiment in the use of extended contact with offenders. Margaret Shaw. 1974. viii + 156pp. (0 11 340122 1) £1.45.

23. Delinquency amongst opiate users. Joy Mott and Marilyn Taylor. 1974. vi + 54pp. (0 11 340663 0) 41p.

†Out of print. Photostat copies can be purchased from Her Majesty's Stationery Office upon request.

24. IMPACT. Intensive matched probation and after-care treatment. Vol. 1. The design of the probation experiment and an interim evaluation. M. S. Folkard, A. J. Fowles, B. C. McWilliams, W. McWilliams, D. D. Smith, D. E. Smith and G. R. Walmsley. 1974. vi + 54pp. (0 11 340664 9) £1.25.

25. The approved school experience. An account of boys' experience of training under differing regimes of approved schools, with an attempt to evaluate the effectiveness of that training. Anne B. Dunlop. 1974. viii + 124pp. (0 11 340665 7). £1.22.

26. Absconding from open prisons. Charlotte Banks, Patricia Mayhew and R. J. Sapsford. 1975. viii + 92pp. (0 11 340666 5) 95p.

27. Driving while disqualified. Sue Kriefman. 1975. vi + 133pp. (0 11 340667 3) £1.22.

28. Some male offenders' problems. I—Homeless offenders in Liverpool. W. McWilliams. II—Casework with short term prisoners. Julie Holborn. 1975. x + 156pp. (0 11 340668 1) £2.50.

29. Community service orders. K. Pease, P. Durkin, I. Earnshaw, D. Payne, J. Thorpe. 1975. viii + 80pp. (0 11 340669 X) 75p.

30. Field Wing Bail Hostel: the first nine months. Frances Simon and Sheena Wilson. 1975. viii + 56pp. (0 11 340670 3) 85p.

31. Homicide in England and Wales 1967 – 1971. Evelyn Gibson. 1975. iv + 60pp. (0 11 340753 X) 90p.

32. Residential treatment and its effects on delinquency. D. B. Cornish and R. V. G. Clarke. 1975. vi + 74pp. (0 11 340672 X) £1.00.

33. Further studies of female offenders. Part A: Borstal girls eight years after release. Nancy Goodman, Elizabeth Maloney and Jean Davies. Part B: The sentencing of women at the London Higher Courts. Nancy Goodman, Paul Durkin and Janet Halron. Part C: Girls appearing before a juvenile court. Jean Davies. 1976. vi + 114pp. (0 11 340673 8) £1.55.

34. Crime as opportunity. P. Mayhew, R. V. G. Clarke, A. Sturman and J. M. Hough. 1976. vii + 36pp. (0 11 340674 6) 70p.

35. The effectiveness of sentencing: a review of the literature. S. R. Brody. 1976. v + 89pp. (0 11 340675 4) £1.15.

36. IMPACT. Intensive matched probation and after-care treatment. Vol. II—The results of the experiment. M. S. Folkard, D. E. Smith and D. D. Smith. 1976. xi + 40pp. (0 11 340676 2) 80p.

37. Police cautioning in England and Wales. J. A. Ditchfield. 1976. iv + 31pp. (0 11 340677 0) 65p.

38. Parole in England and Wales. C. P. Nuttall, with E. E. Barnard, A. J. Fowles, A. Frost, W. H. Hammond, P. Mayhew, K. Pease, R. Tarling and M. J. Weatheritt. 1977. vi + 90pp. (0 11 340678 9) £1.75.

39. Community service assessed in 1976. K. Pease, S. Billingham and I. Earnshaw. 1977. vi + 29pp. (0 11 340679 7) 75p.

40. Screen violence and film censorship. Stephen Brody. 1977. vi + 179pp. (0 11 340680 0) £2.75.

41. Absconding from borstals. Gloria K. Laycock. 1977. v + 82pp. (0 11 340681 9) £1.50.

42. Gambling—a review of the literature and its implications for policy and research. D. B. Cornish. 1978. xii + 284pp. (0 11 340682 7) £4.25.

43. Compensation orders in magistrates' courts. Paul Softley. 1978. vi + 41pp. (0 11 340683 5) 90p.

44. Research in criminal justice. John Croft. 1978. vi + 16pp. (0 11 340684 3) 50p.

45. Prison welfare: an account of an experiment at Liverpool. A. J. Fowles. 1978. v + 34pp. (0 11 340685 1) 75p.

46. Fines in magistrates' courts. Paul Softley. 1978. v + 42pp. (0 11 340686 X) £1.00.

47. Tackling vandalism. R. V. G. Clarke (editor), F. J. Gladstone, A. Sturman, Sheena Wilson (contributors). 1978. vi + 91pp. (0 11 340687 8) £2.00.

48. Social inquiry reports: a survey. Jennifer Thorpe. 1979. vi + 55pp. (0 11 340688 6) £1.50.

49. Crime in public view. P. Mayhew, R. V. G. Clarke, J. N. Burrows, J. M. Hough, S. W. C. Winchester. 1979. v + 36pp. (0 11 340689 4) £1.00.

50. Crime and the community. John Croft. 1979. v + 16pp. (0 11 340690 8) 65p.

51. Life-sentence prisoners. David Smith (editor), Christopher Brown, Joan Worth, Roger Sapsford, Charlotte Banks (contributors). 1979. 56pp. (0 11 340691 6) £1.25.

52. Hostels for offenders. Jane E. Andrews with an appendix by Bill Sheppard. 1979. 36pp. (0 11 340692 4) £1.50.

53. Previous convictions, sentence and reconviction: a statistical study of a sample of 5,000 offenders convicted in January 1971. G. J. O. Phillpotts and L. B. Lancucki. 1979. 60pp. (0 11 340693 2) £2.25.

54. Sexual offences, consent and sentencing. Roy Walmsley and Karen White. 1979. 83pp. (0 11 340694 0) £2.75.

HMSO

Government publications can be purchased from the Government Bookshops at the addresses listed on cover page iv (post orders to PO Box 569, London SE1 9NH) or through booksellers.

Printed in England for Her Majesty's Stationery Office by Hobbs the Printers of Southampton
(1876) Dd0599707 K16 11/79 G327